MYSTERIOUS CASTLE BUILDERS: AFRICAN TERMITES

by
Tom Lisker

cpi
contemporary perspectives, inc.

This book is distributed by Silver Burdett Company, Morristown, New Jersey 07960.

Library of Congress Number: 78-21886

Art and Photo Credits
Cover photo, Glenn D. Prestwich
Photos on pages 4, 10, 15, 21, 27, 29, 30, 34, 36, 38, 41, 42, and 44, Glenn D.
    Prestwich
Illustrations on pages 6, 9, 13, 17, 18, 33, and 47, Beverly Wallace. Reprinted
    courtesy of Coronet Instructional Media, a division of Esquire, Inc.
Photo on page 22, Dr. Howard Topoff
Illustrations on pages 21, 22, and 25, David Morris
Every effort has been made to trace the ownership of all copyrighted material in this
    book and obtain permission for its use.

Library of Congress Cataloging in Publication Data

Lisker, Tom, 1928-
    The mysterious castle builders — African termites.

    Bibliography: p.
    SUMMARY: Discusses the life cycle of African termites, cellulose-eating insects
living in very rigid societies housed in giant pyramids of mud or sand.
    1. Termites — African — Juvenile literature. 2. Insects — Africa — Juvenile
literature. [1. Termites. 2. Insects] I. Title
QL529.26.A1L57   595.7'36   78-21886
ISBN 0-89547-074-8

Manufactured in the United States of America
ISBN 0-89547-074-8

CONTENTS

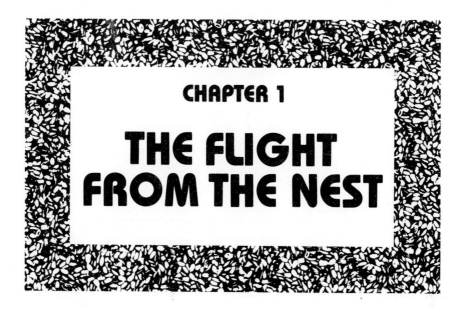

CHAPTER 1

THE FLIGHT FROM THE NEST

Night falls quickly on the African plain. Soon it is too dark for many daytime animals to see. But when the sun sets, other creatures come out. A whole strange and different world springs to life.

It is March in East Africa's Great Rift Valley, and the "big rains" are beginning. For nearly half a year there has been no rain. The land has grown dry. It is red and cracked from the fierce heat of the sun. The animals are even thirstier than the people. There is almost nothing left to drink in their water holes.

At last, though, the rain begins to pound on the earth, sinking into the dry ground. Tonight there will

◄ Rising from the African plains, looking like giant sand castles, are the nests of the termites.

5

The first rain in months brings the young termites from the nest.

be plenty of water. But the animals of the night are interested in more than water. They are waiting for the march of the termites. Tonight the young termites will leave their nest for the first time. The animals will have more than just water to drink. They will have food to eat. They will feast on insects — thousands and thousands of young termites.

Why do millions of termites risk their lives by flying from the nest? What happens on this rainy night is part of a mystery that is almost as old as the earth itself. It is the story of that tiny, mysterious creature, the termite.

Termites are sometimes called white ants, but they're not really ants at all! Many of them do crawl on the ground like ordinary ants. Some of these termites are known as soldiers, and some are called workers. But many other termites have wings and can fly. They all live together in nests.

The termites' nest is called a *termitary*, and it is like nothing else in the world. It is built of sand and mud. Some termitaries are as tall as two-story houses. But they don't look anything like houses. Many nests make you think of giant castles with great archways and high towers!

When you first see a termitary, you might wonder why it can't be easily knocked over by larger animals. Impossible! The nest is as hard and as strong as rock. That's important because a million termites can live in one nest. And on this rainy night, each one of those termites seems to know that something special is about to happen.

For hours the wingless worker termites have been digging holes in the walls of the nest. When their job is done, thousands of other termites will come pouring out of the mud-and-sand house.

The winged termites have never seen the world outside. But each of these winged creatures has been waiting for this chance to fly into that unknown world!

Finally the workers finish. Holes have been dug through the thick sides of the nest. The soldiers are the first to come out. With their big, strong jaws they have to fight off any enemy insects nearby.

Then the first winged termites make their way through the openings. For a minute or two they stand at the edge of the nest. They try to see where they are, but the night is too dark. They can see nothing. And even though they have wings, they haven't learned to fly yet!

Slowly they move their wings, trying to get into the air. But their wings seem too weak to lift them even an inch!

Now they become excited. They crowd each other at the openings of the nest. Then one by one they jump from the holes! Now they *must* learn to fly!

Most of the termites lift their wings weakly and fly for only a second or two. Then they must crawl down the sides of the nest. But others are able to fly to the ground. Some of the stronger termites even fly a few feet farther. They land on leaves or blades of grass. But even the strongest termites can't fly much farther than a few hundred yards from the nest.

Meanwhile, the workers inside the termitary have a new job. Quickly, but carefully, they fill the holes in

Thousands of young termites become a "feast" for the creatures who live on the plain.

the sides of the nest. It's the way they "lock" the doors! No creature can get into the nest now, not even any of the thousands and thousands of termites that have just left. They can never return to their home.

Most of them won't have the chance to return anyway. Even before the nest is sealed off, birds, mice, snakes, frogs, and spiders have begun their feast. In less than an hour nearly all of the winged

termites have been eaten. Out of hundreds of thousands, only a few dozen are left!

But those few termites have a job to do. They must now find mates and breed more termites. Those termites that survive will build nests that reach deep into the ground. They will pile up soil, grain by grain, until it forms the giant "castles" that dot the African plain. And in their termitaries they will set up a "society" — a way of life — as ordered as any ever set up by people.

But first these few termites must make sure that they will survive. It is up to them to keep alive one of the oldest and most mysterious worlds on earth.

◄ Worker termites build their sand-castle nests by piling up grains of sand, one at a time.

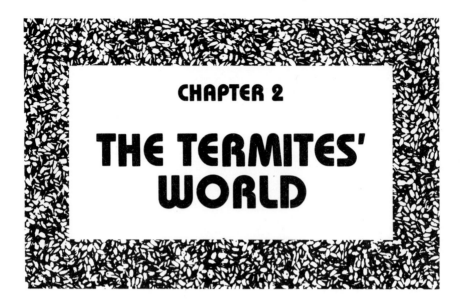

CHAPTER 2

THE TERMITES' WORLD

The termites that escape will keep their world alive. But in many ways their flight seems almost senseless. Thousands and thousands of termites have tried to fly from their nest. Swarming out, they look like bits of paper or snow falling *up* instead of down! Although their wings are a beautiful sight, those wings can hardly carry the termites at all. And only a few of these insects live more than a few minutes after their short flight. They are quickly caught and gobbled up!

Why do they do it? What makes the termites go on this flight? For years *entomologists* (scientists who

Flying termites fill the air like flakes of snow.

study insects) have asked the same question. They want to know why termites build their giant nests and why they fly from these nests. But entomologists can only guess at the reasons.

First of all, what makes the termites leave the nest? Some people think that they leave to build a *new* nest. The termitary may have gotten old and weak. And the termites themselves might have

13

become old too. If just one male and female stay alive after a flight, they can breed millions of new termites. These *stronger* termites will build new termitaries.

But there might be an even more important reason for the termites' flight. Nature often has a way of choosing the strongest creatures to stay alive. The famous naturalist Charles Darwin called this "the survival of the fittest."

The termites that can fly far enough and fast enough will survive. These termites will mate and become the parents of young termites. The new termites will be stronger and healthier than the earlier ones. In this way each flight from the nest leads to stronger termites. *These* termites will be better able to escape the other creatures of the African bush.

Scientists also ask why termites choose one special rainy night to fly from the termitary. How do they know it is raining outside the nest? How can they tell when it's night? Why should thousands of workers, all at once, begin to make holes in the walls of their nest? Who or *what* tells the soldier termites to fight off enemy insects? Does one termite give some kind of order? Why do the termites left inside the nest fill in the holes after the other termites have gone? Can scientists answer these questions? Perhaps not. And there are even greater mysteries about these termites!

Inside the termitary only the winged termites have "eyes" and "ears." The worker and the soldier termites can never see or hear. They do not even seem to have a sense of smell. The world of the termites is one of the oldest on earth. How does it work if most of the termites are blind and deaf? Are sight and hearing not really needed by the termites?

Many scientists think that termites learn in a very special way. The worker and soldier termites seem to be able to "feel" the world around them. When a creature walks or flies past, "shock waves" are set off in the ground or air. Scientists believe that the blind and deaf termites can feel these waves!

More surprising, even though worker and soldier termites can't see, they can *feel* light. They feel when the sun is shining. And they even seem to be able to feel the light from a flashlight.

Maybe the most mysterious of these creatures is the termite queen. Scientists believe that the queen rules the termitary. She seems to have a strange power over everything. If "orders" are given to the other termites, they are probably given by the queen. But she does not give these orders with words — or even with signs. Somehow the queen uses the *chemicals* in all the termites' bodies to tell the others what to do!

How do we know about the queen's power? In experiments scientists have taken the queen out of the termitary. When this is done *everything in the nest stops!* Workers stop working. Soldiers stop fighting off the nest's enemies. Even the queen's eggs shrivel up. Sometimes a few termites will escape and join other nests. But the rest just seem to stop living.

With a twist of her body, the queen throws off her wings forever.

And how does a female termite become a queen? When she flies from the nest, the female begins to act in a strange way. As soon as she has landed on the ground she gives her body a single twist, and her wings come off! Then she stands very still. Somehow she is able to signal male termites. She makes no

The queen and her king begin digging their nest in the soft ground.

special sound or call. But the males learn where she is. Scientists believe they can find her because she gives off a kind of "royal perfume" that only queens and their future mates can smell.

Male termites find the females by following these signals. When a male reaches a female, he touches her

18

with a long, skinny feeler that sticks out of his head like a TV antenna. As soon as she is touched, the female runs away. The male runs right after her! But the female isn't trying to escape.

Then why does she bother to run away at all? Scientists think that the strange chase is really a kind of "house hunting." The termites must find a place where they will be safe from the hungry creatures that want to eat them. And they must find this place fast! As soon as the female finds a spot, she starts digging into the damp earth. The ground, softened by the rain, is easy to dig. Sometimes the male helps her dig. But usually he just watches.

When the female has dug an inch or two below the surface, she makes a small "room" half an inch wide. Then both termites crawl in. They quickly close the hole from the inside. They stay there several months. For a while they will be safe.

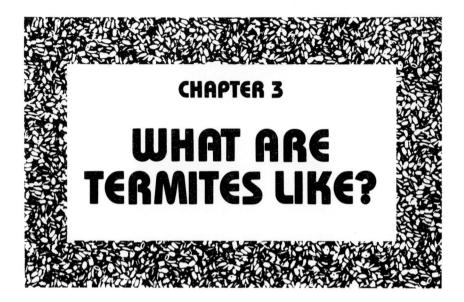

CHAPTER 3

WHAT ARE TERMITES LIKE?

What happens during those months when the termites are buried in that hole under the ground? Why do the male termite and the queen stay there so long? To understand what is happening, we should know more about what termites are like. To begin, the mysterious African termites are only one of the many different kinds of termites. There are over 2,000 kinds, or *species*, of termites. They seem to live in almost every part of the world.

But humans don't seem to know much about them. For example, you have already found out that termites are often called "white ants," even though they're *not* ants and are not really white. Termites, though, are

A Worker Termite

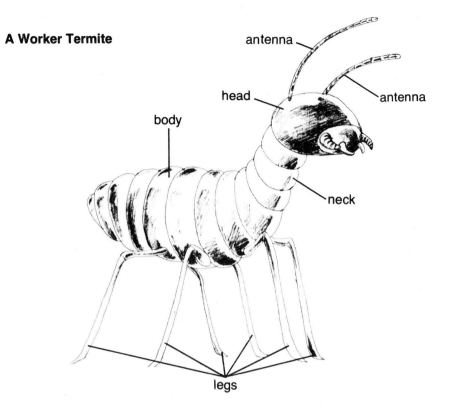

antenna

head

antenna

body

neck

legs

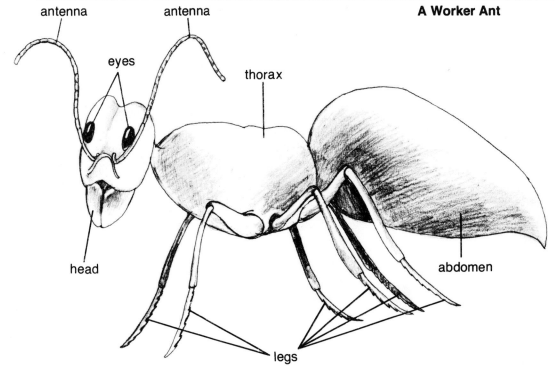

A Worker Ant

antenna

antenna

eyes

thorax

head

abdomen

legs

22

about the same size as ants. And like ants they live in groups called *colonies*. But ants and termites are very different. Ants and termites do not even look very much alike. The termite has only a head, a neck, and a large body. But the ant also has a "chest" and a "waist."

The two insects don't grow in the same way either. Ants go through a number of stages as they grow. First they are *eggs*, then *larvae* (LÄŔ-VĒ), *pupae* (PYŬ-PĒ), and finally grown-up *ants*.

The termite's life is very different. When the egg hatches, what comes out is a *termite*! In fact it looks just like a fully grown termite, only smaller. To grow, the termite just sheds its skin. After it does this five or six times, the termite has become an adult!

There are many other differences between ants and termites. But one of the most important is the outer *shell*. Ants have a hard crust around their bodies very much like a suit of armor. This makes their bodies hard and tough to protect them from other creatures. But termites' bodies have no shell and are very soft. Maybe that's why many creatures would rather eat termites than ants!

Termites really have no way to defend themselves from the creatures that like to eat them. So they have to spend most of their lives hiding! Some termites live underground. Others live in their strong termitary. This is why many termites never see the light of day. In fact, only the winged termites ever really go outside. And even *they* go out only when it is dark!

Once they are hidden in their nest the termites build almost a whole world of their own. This world is as neat and organized as the world of human beings. Some scientists say that termites are even more organized than people!

The termitary is just one example of how organized the termites really are. The termitary is made up of many different "rooms." Each is used for a special job, and is made to help the termites survive and grow. In a termitary the part that rises above the ground protects the termites from their enemies. The actual nest is below this. In it are different places for growing the termites' food. In other parts of the nest the young termites are fed and raised. And deep inside the heart of the nest is the pair of royal termites, the king and queen.

Each of these different sections is like a separate "apartment" inside the termitary. And the apartments are connected by tunnels. But these tunnels do more than help the termites get from one "apartment" to another. They also keep the termitary comfortable for the termites! Like a natural air conditioner, the

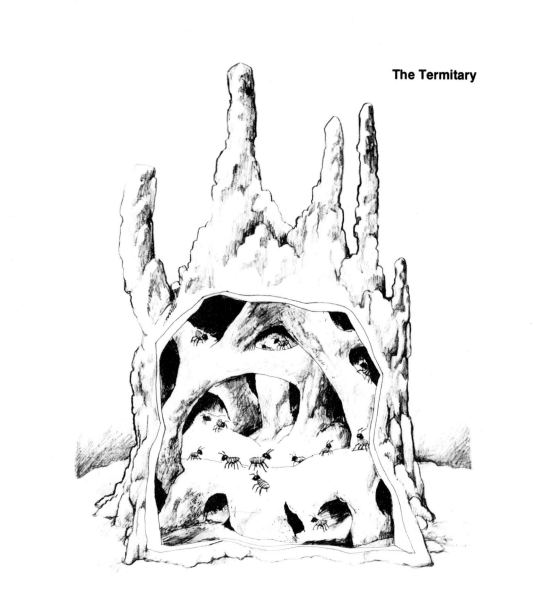

tunnels govern the temperature and even the amount of moisture in the air.

The termites are just as organized. There are three main groups of termites in a nest — workers, soldiers, and winged termites that can become kings and queens. Each termite is born with a special job to do, and it will do that job until it dies! Maybe that's why its body has all the special parts it needs in order to do that one job.

Not only are termites very organized. They also have very long lives — for insects. A housefly usually lives only a month or so, but king and queen termites often live 20 years. The workers and soldiers don't live quite that long. But as long as they *are* alive, the workers and soldiers never stop doing their jobs. They toil 24 hours a day, seven days a week. In spite of this they still manage to live for half a year. In the insect world that's a ripe old age!

One reason termites live so long is what they eat — their diet. Termites eat *cellulose.* Cellulose is a chemical that is found in plants and trees. But you also can find it in just about anything that has ever been alive. It is even found in things that are *made* from things that have been alive. Wood, seeds, rags, and paper all have cellulose in them.

This makes cellulose a very special and useful food. A creature that lives on cellulose can eat just about anything and never run out of food! Because of this diet, the termite has survived on earth for millions of years.

Cellulose is so important to termites that, in some nests, they even have "gardens" for growing this food.

Termites eat the cellulose in special ways. In the stomachs of many kinds of termites are millions and millions of tiny creatures. These creatures are called *protozoans*, and they live by eating cellulose. Some kinds of termite workers chew and swallow the cellulose in any food they can find. Then the millions of protozoans inside the workers' stomachs "eat" the cellulose for the termites!

Other kinds of termites eat in an even more surprising way. The termites that build nests in the African bush do not have protozoans to eat for them. The African termites build little gardens inside their nests! In them the termites plant a tiny white *fungus*, something very much like a small mushroom. The fungus grows by "eating" cellulose the termites have brought into the termitary. Then the termites eat the fungus!

Human beings usually think of the termite as one of the "most wanted criminals" in the animal world. Many people believe that all that termites really do is ruin and destroy. In some cases this is true. The Formosan termite, for example, has been called one of the most destructive insects on earth. It was first found on the island of Formosa. Since then this termite has traveled to Hawaii and even as far as New Orleans. Wherever it has gone it has eaten cellulose. Planted fields and even wooden houses have been ruined!

African termites, however, are different. Their work does not always bring such ruin. These termites, in fact, are one of the most important parts of life in Africa. One reason is that there are no earthworms to turn over the dry clay of the African plain. That important job is left to the termites. The termites also have the task of "recycling" dead wood that lies on the ground. They take the cellulose of this rotting wood and make it useful for farming.

As they dig, the termites turn over the ground and make it fit for fungus farming.

More important, termites are food not just for animals, but for people. When it is not raining, African children strike the sides of termitaries with brooms. The termites inside "feel" this sound and think it's

A group of African children near a termitary, from which they will drive the termites.

raining outside! As they fly from their nest, they are quickly gathered up by the children. Buckets filled with termites are then taken home or carried to the market for sale.

Termites can be eaten just as they are, or they can be cooked in many different ways. Today termites are even fried, salted, put in plastic bags, and sold all over the world!

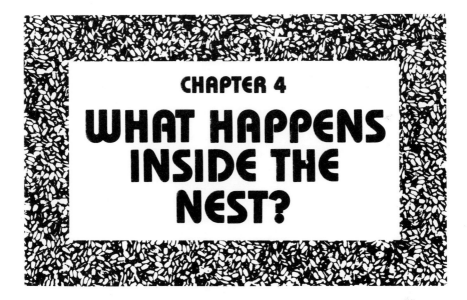

CHAPTER 4
WHAT HAPPENS INSIDE THE NEST?

Since termites are eaten by so many different creatures it is surprising that there are any termites left at all. But scientists tell us that termites have been around for over a hundred million years! That means that termites have been around about ten times longer than people! Somehow *some* termites always manage to survive and breed more termites.

How have termites been able to go on for so long? One reason is that they eat cellulose. There is almost always food for termites. Just as important, millions of termites hatch and fly from their nests every year.

Only a few survive that first flight from a nest. But millions of other termites are always born.

The African termites' nest begins with the king and queen. These two termites have escaped from the old nest without being eaten. The king has followed the queen's royal perfume until the two termites have found a place for their new nest. Then they bury themselves underground. There the royal pair will sleep through the winter.

When spring comes the royal pair awake and mate. But now they have a great deal of work to do. Their first job is to get water for the nest. They will have to dig far down into the wet earth. Working in darkness, the royal pair will work day and night underground until they find the water they need.

Once this has been done the two termites have an even bigger job. They must now plant their garden of fungus. This will be the food supply for the whole termitary.

They begin building this garden by chewing dry wood and grass until it is broken into small pieces. After they mix these pieces with water, they use the mixture to cover the ground and walls of their nest. Now the termites start planting their garden with fungus seeds they have brought with them from the old nest.

The termite queen digs into the earth to find water for the new nest she is building.

When this fungus garden is ready, the queen will lay her first eggs. The queen studies the nest as if looking for the best place for her babies. At first she moves all the time. Then she suddenly stops, lifting her body up in the air. At last, the queen is laying her eggs.

Worker and soldier termites surround their queen, who has now grown thousands of times larger than any of them.

Like most insects, the female termite lays thousands of eggs at a time. But unlike many other insects, the female termite stays with her eggs. She lies beside her eggs, touching them gently with her jaws and front legs. She does this right up until the time they hatch. The king termite also stays with the eggs. After the eggs are laid he moves over beside the queen. If the royal room is attacked he will try to save the queen and her eggs.

When the first eggs are laid the king and queen are about the same size. But as the years go by the queen gets larger and larger. Some queens will grow to 5,000 times the size they were when they flew from the old nest! But all through the years the "tiny" king stays at the queen's side, taking care of her.

The first eggs hatch and from them come the blind and deaf workers. The king and queen care for these young workers. The babies soon will take over the job of running the termitary.

When these young workers grow up they do the jobs around the nest the royal couple had been doing. They dig for water and plant gardens of fungus. They even chew the grass and wood that keep the nest safe and solid. These workers also take care of the eggs and babies that come later. The workers feed everybody — even the royal couple.

Once the workers begin their job the queen lays another group of eggs. These will become the soldier termites. Like the workers they will be blind and deaf. But the smaller soldiers are able to protect the edges of the nest, while the larger soldiers guard the queen.

The soldiers are quite different from the workers. In the first place they have pincers (claws) 500 times the size of the workers' jaws! They use these to attack

intruders trying to break into the nest. The soldiers are strong enough — and fierce enough — to drive off many unwelcome visitors.

Some termite soldiers defend the nest with weapons even more powerful than jaws and pincers. In Australia there also are termites that build tall nests. The soldiers of these nests have a strange and deadly way of fighting. They have heads that look like tiny spray guns. When an enemy comes near the nest, it is met with sprays of poison from these soldiers' "squirt guns." The poison surrounds the enemy like a net. Trapped and unable to breathe, the termites' enemy soon dies.

These Australian termites have another weapon — messages. When an enemy attacks, it is met by a group of soldiers. This first group sends a chemical message to other soldiers in the termitary. Soon these other soldiers are on the march. All of these termite soldiers are blind and deaf. But they all spray their deadly poison at anything that attacks the nest.

But the soldier termites of both Australia and Africa are unable to feed themselves! They must get all their food from the workers. Sometimes the workers decide the nest has too many soldiers. When this happens, the workers just stop feeding them. Soon the soldiers starve, and the termite army becomes smaller. This is

◄ This soldier's pincers will be used over and over to protect the termites' nest from insect enemies.

The workers take liquid food from the queen to feed the baby termites.

how the termites in the termitary keep their nest from getting too crowded.

Meanwhile the queen keeps growing. The termitary and the number of termites keep growing too. That means that more and more water must be found, new tunnels must be dug, and new gardens must be planted. The food must be harvested too. For the worker termites, work never stops.

As they carry out their jobs the workers take more and more soil, one bit at a time, to the nest. Soon a mound rises well above ground level. After the termitary has grown this large, the queen lays more eggs. From these will hatch the winged termites that may become kings and queens. When these termites fly from the nest the cycle of termite life will start all over again.

By this time the queen has become a kind of egg-laying machine. In fact she produces as many as 30,000 eggs each day! But she is locked inside her dark royal chamber. The queen has grown too large to ever crawl back through the hole she made so long ago!

Thousands of worker termites keep busy feeding the queen with drops of liquid food. Other workers pick up her eggs and carry them to the place where they will hatch. Meanwhile smaller workers keep touching the queen's huge body. They do this until they get tiny drops of a special liquid. They carry this away and use it to feed the baby termites.

All this time a ring of soldiers stands around the queen. These are the largest and strongest of the termite soldiers. It is their duty to protect the queen and her eggs. But at different times other soldiers move in to take their place. Then the first ring of soldiers leaves and is replaced by these new guards.

Most of the time the queen's special soldiers just stand around her, never moving. But sometimes they do strange things. Every once in a while one of them starts rocking back and forth. That soldier seems to excite the others. Pretty soon all of them are slowly moving around the queen in a strange dance. Why do they do this? Even scientists aren't sure.

What goes on if something unusual happens in the nest? Once an entomologist watched as a piece of dirt fell from the ceiling of the nest. It landed on the queen. It must have hit her very hard. The queen began to swing her head back and forth. Her soldiers quickly disappeared. Then the workers stopped feeding her. They surrounded her, as if they were trying to take away the milky liquid in her body.

In a few minutes the queen's skin started to hang down. It looked as if she would not live much longer. Meanwhile all the other termites seemed to have forgotten their jobs. The organization of the termitary seemed to be falling apart!

But then, slowly, the queen began to gather back her strength. As she grew stronger the workers started to return. Once again they fed her. In a few hours the queen grew back to her usual size. Within a day every termite in the termitary was working just as before. Everything seemed to be back to normal.

The nursery is one of the busiest places in the termitary. ▶

Chemicals in the queen's body seem to direct everything that happens within the termite nest.

But why had the soldiers run off when the queen needed them? Wasn't their job to protect and try to save her? After all, the queen is the very heart of the nest. She seems to control everything that happens in the termitary. What changed when the termite queen was hurt? Had she lost that strange chemical power that tells the other termites what to do? And what brought the soldiers and workers back to her side? How did they know that the queen once again was healthy?

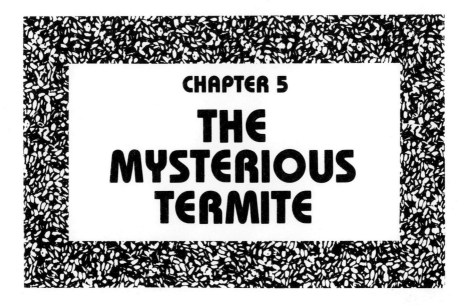

CHAPTER 5

THE MYSTERIOUS TERMITE

How and why the soldiers and workers protect the queen is not the only mystery about the termite. Strangely, of all the creatures on earth the termite would seem to be one of the least important and least mysterious. To many people termites are only pests that ruin houses, destroy forests, or even eat their way through books. To many other people termites are a nice snack!

But the tiny termite turns out to be one of the most interesting creatures in the world, with a life as

organized and complicated as our own. For example, the termite is small, blind, and deaf, but it can build a curved arch. This is something people learned how to do only after thousands of years!

How does the termite make this arch? Worker termites first build two columns. The columns are not very tall and they are only a few inches apart. Then a worker climbs up one of the columns, carrying a blade of grass. The worker sticks one end of the piece of grass to the top of the column. Then the worker lets the blade of grass fall across to the other column.

More worker termites are waiting for the grass to land on that column. Quickly they attach the end of the blade of grass to *their* column. On this piece of grass the termites stick tiny pebbles. Stone by stone they build the arch higher and higher. Finally, after long, difficult work, a perfect arch is built.

Scientists studied one termitary that weighed *23,500 pounds*, nearly 12 tons! It took hundreds of years to build, one tiny piece of earth at a time.

The termites' digging and building can make them useful to people. For example, can you picture mining for gold in termite mounds? Well, termites are helping find gold in the southern African country of Rhodesia.

◀ Scientists seek to solve the mysteries within the termitary.

Just like termites everywhere else, termites in Rhodesia need water in order to survive. To find that water they will dig hundreds of feet into the ground. As they tunnel through the earth, the termites carry dirt back up to the surface, one grain at a time. This is the dirt that helps build the tall mounds of the African termitaries. There are thousands and thousands of these mounds in Rhodesia. Many of them are in the Kalahari sands.

Nearly half the Rhodesian land that could be used for mining gold is covered by Kalahari sands. The shifting sand makes it almost impossible to mine for gold in the usual way. Miners' shafts and tunnels simply collapse when they are dug into the sand. So many miners now have termites do their prospecting for them.

Rhodesian miners study the earth termites bring to the surface. From it they learn what minerals lie below the surface. If they find gold, they can thank their termite "prospectors" for it! In Rhodesia the miners and government have studied thousands of termite mounds. And they have found gold with the help of the termites.

Unfortunately, not all the work of termites is so useful. In North America termites cause $200,000,000 worth of damage every year. Termites are at work everywhere except the coldest parts of North America.

As they tunnel through the earth, termites sometimes bring up bits of gold.

They're probably at work right in your neighborhood. You may not see them or hear them. But you often can see where they have been and what they have done.

North American termites do not build the tall mounds of the African termites. But they do act much the same. They live on cellulose — which means they'll eat just about any plant or anything made from a plant. These termites will eat books, suitcases, wallpaper, clothes, papers put in metal cabinets, and even money kept in bank vaults!

47

But not all termites are so harmful to people. In fact, as we have learned over the years, the African termite is one of the most valuable creatures in the land. The strange, beautiful mounds that rise above the African plain show their work.

The mysterious life of these creatures goes on all the time. Every day and night the African termites quietly work under and above the earth. Most of us don't even know what they're doing or why.

In fact, we probably know more about the planets of outer space than we know about this tiny world of creatures on our own planet!